T0160499

Grace *and* Frankie

© 2021 Skydance Productions LLC. All Rights Reserved.

No part of this book may be reproduced, or stored in a retrieval system, or transmitted in any form or by any means, electronic, mechanical, photocopying, recording, or otherwise, without express written permission of the publisher.

Published by Flashpoint™ Books, Seattle
www.flashpointbooks.com

Produced by Girl Friday Productions
www.girlfridayproductions.com

Written by Emilie Sandoz-Voyer
Illustrations by Emma Russell

Design: Paul Barrett
Photo research: Micah Schmidt
Development & editorial: Kristin Mehus-Roe, Georgie Hockett, and Leslie Miller
Production editorial: Tiffany Taing and Dave Valencia

Photographs from "Grace and Frankie" courtesy of Skydance Productions, LLC. All rights reserved. © Netflix [2015–2020]. Used with permission.

ISBN: 978-1-7363243-8-7

Library of Congress Control Number: 2021936164

First edition

Grace *and* Frankie

A GUIDE TO BEST-FRIENDSHIP
and NOT GIVING A DAMN

By Emilie Sandoz-Voyer

Foreword by Co-creators
Marta Kauffman
and **Howard J. Morris**

FLASH
POINT

CONTENTS

FOREWORD 6
INTRODUCTION 8

Chapter 1
THROUGH THICK AND THIN 12

Chapter 2
TRUE WORKMANCE 38

Chapter 3
REAL FRIENDS FIGHT 62

Chapter 4
ROMANCE IS OVERRATED 88

Chapter 5
GOOD FRIENDS LAST FOREVER 116

ACKNOWLEDGMENTS 144

True story: At a fortuitous lunch, Marta Kauffman heard that Jane Fonda and Lily Tomlin wanted to do television. Marta thought it meant they wanted to do a show together. After calling her agent to find out if this was true, the agent said, "I'll call you back." Twenty minutes later, she got a call back saying, "They do now."

Another true story: Marta Kauffman called Howard J. Morris and said, "I want to do a show about sexuality in older women, so naturally I thought of you." And Howard said "I'm in" without thinking about it. And he still hasn't thought about it, eight years and ninety-four episodes later. All he knows is she called him, and when she told him it was with Jane Fonda and Lily Tomlin, he realized he was the luckiest person in the world—and he's really glad he didn't screen her call!

As we write this foreword, we are wrapping up *Grace and Frankie* after seven seasons. It's very hard to say goodbye to this show that has meant so much to us, and even more painful to say goodbye to all the wonderful people we've had the opportunity to work with over these years. It's especially hard to end *Grace and Frankie*, because our show is about beginnings. It's about starting over. And then starting over again. And when you think it's really the end this time, it's about finding a way to start over one more time.

And the only way Grace and Frankie are able to do this is with the guidance and support of each other. And who better to portray a great friendship than long time, real-life friends Jane Fonda and Lily Tomlin? It doesn't hurt that they both also happen to be legends and their off-screen chemistry is as potent as it is on-screen. But *Grace and Frankie* isn't only about Grace and Frankie. It's also about all the people in their lives. We've been blessed to work with an unbelievably talented cast, including two other legends, Martin Sheen and Sam

Waterston. There are also several legends in the making: June Diane Raphael, Brooklyn Decker, Baron Vaughn, and Ethan Embry.

When we started the show, there were a lot of questions, the biggest one being, if you are doing a show about people in their seventies, will only people in their seventies watch? The answer was very clearly no. We have been shocked, amazed, and grateful to see people of all ages embracing the show and these characters. It has been especially rewarding for us to see how our audience has been able to relate to a story about two friends overcoming divorces, dry vaginas, and all the other indignities of aging.

And whether you're a Grace needing a Frankie, or a Frankie needing a Grace, the good news is she can walk into your life at any time. But until then, keep streaming.

Lastly, thank you to our fans for making us the longest running show on Netflix.

—Co-creators Marta and Howard

HOWARD J. MORRIS

INTRODUCTION

I f you've already planned the communal space where you and your best friend will live out your golden years, have a friend who knows just what you meant to say (even when you're not quite sure what it was), or have realized that the best Saturday-night date can't compare with the adventures the two of you get up to, then this book is for you.

It's for all the Graces and Frankies out there who choose each other rather than the yam farmers and billionaires; who can be counted on to pull each other off the toilet or join one another on the floor; who know that, in a jam, they'd rather call each other than anyone else.

Being best friends doesn't mean you always agree with each other. In fact, you might disagree dramatically and memorably. But your love for each other is rooted in the nugget of sameness that lies within. Take Mountain Dew and black coffee. Their flavor profiles couldn't be more different, but deep down they share something essential—the power to caffeinate the hell out of you. True friendship is like that.

Maybe, like Grace and Frankie themselves, your bond was forged in the fires of shared suffering. Or maybe it has been the slow build of years of shared jokes and friendly disagreements about where to store your hats (hat rack, or dishwasher?). However you came together, and however confounding your friendship may seem to everyone else, you love one another, quirks and all.

In a world where everything we do feels like one big setup to get into or stay in romantic relationships, Grace and Frankie turn that upside down. What if you and your favorite person could reinvent yourselves and completely start over—together—and dare to do all those things you spent so many years telling yourself you couldn't?

This book is a celebration of best-friendship, in all its imperfection and glory. Take the quizzes, follow the tips, make the recipes—aspire to be the

greatest Grace or Frankie you can be. Don't give a damn how the world sees you, because remember, if they can't see you, they can't catch you. And don't worry about finding your dream partner, because your bestie sees you just fine. Your soul mate isn't around the corner, they're already with you—sharing a metaphorical La Jolla beach house, finishing your sentences even when they're gibberish, and keeping you strong.

ARE YOU A GRACE OR A FRANKIE?

1. What do you look for in a friend?

    a. A mad genius brain, even if it's hidden below more unruly hair than anyone has the right to possess.

    b. A warm heart, even if it's hidden within a body that's essentially an ice sculpture of a whippet.

2. What would you say is your best quality as a friend?

    a. Executive functioning—you can prep, cook, and serve a dinner for ten with military precision *and* teach your roommate to fold a fitted sheet.

    b. Emotional availability—whether it's an on-demand vision quest, an endless willingness to engage in a sharing circle, or a heart as open as a twenty-four-hour Del Taco.

3. What do you dislike in a friend?

    a. Meddling—please keep your nose in your own business and leave my martini at the door.

    b. A closed mind—if you're not operating on more than one astral plane, what are you even doing?

4. What do you bring to a friend who is struggling?

    a. Space.

    b. Pot, a veggie-works burrito, and your whole damn self.

5. What's the best gift you've ever received?

  a. A couch stuffed with cash.

  b. A hot-air-balloon ride. Though if anyone's looking to shop for you anytime soon, you have had your eye on a three-day conscious touch workshop in Joshua Tree. The vagina painting studio is supposed to be life changing!

6. What's the best gift you've ever given?

  a. Your time. It's not priceless, but most people can't afford it.

  b. Your love. It *is* priceless, but there's always enough to go around, and you're handing it out like candy.

Mostly A's: You're a Grace! Popped collar, perfect makeup, and an icy stare that can stop a person's blood in their veins. You may be intimidating, but you are fiercely loyal and have deep (and very private) reserves of emotion for your closest friends.

Mostly B's: You're a Frankie! You're as loose and relaxed as an extra-large Grateful Dead T-shirt, and you will always be there for a friend—though you may be a little late if you had to stop for fro-yo along the way.

CHAPTER 1

THROUGH THICK AND THIN

"I'm the glue that keeps that vintage Barbie together."

—FRANKIE

Life may include losses, but having a Grace or Frankie can help take the sting out of even the worst existential crisis. From the celebratory goodbye (the big goodbye) party for their best friend, Babe, to their banishment to a retirement community by their well-meaning children and the temporary sale of their beloved beach house, Grace and Frankie face loss in the most appropriate of ways: with a middle finger to the past.

It's when shit gets real that Grace and Frankie really show up for each other, even if showing up sometimes looks suspiciously like taking a nap. They're each other's wing woman at funerals and their exes' wedding and they support each other through medical crises and housing disasters. When life gets them down (or, you know, when Grace really just can't get up), they are there for each other.

If you have a friend who knows when LOL means SOS and will bail you out of any jam, as deserved as the jam might be, then you are already on the path of greatness—a Grace and Frankie soul connection.

HOW TO SUPPORT YOUR BOSOM BUDDY

Frankie's Comfort Top Ten

1. Talking it out . . . at a silent retreat
2. Cheese, nacho cheese, shredded cheese, parmesan, and queso.
3. Exploring the depth of the universe through crafting.
4. Neuropathy socks
5. Laughter yoga
6. Starbursts
7. Bongos
8. Gummy worm edibles
9. Quesadilla-stuffed quesadillas
10. Grace

Grace's Comfort Top Ten

1. A problem that needs fixing
2. Getting carded
3. Ménage à Moi
4. A good comeback line
5. Control
6. Judging strangers with Mallory and Brianna
7. The full line of Say Grace products
8. A packed weekly schedule
9. Just a whisper of Botox
10. Frankie

"DAMN my Christlike capacity for COMPASSION."

—*Frankie*

Any problem can be solved with the right tools.

FRANKIE: You know what this situation needs?

GRACE: Don't say fondue—

FRANKIE: Fondue.

Quesadilla-Stuffed Quesadilla

What's the best comfort food? A quesadilla, of course: a warm tortilla wrapped in a loving embrace with a mound of gooey cheese. But when you really need to up the ante to soothe your emotional bruises, how about two quesadillas holding on to each other for dear life?

INGREDIENTS

- ½ cup shredded cheddar cheese
- ½ cup shredded jack cheese
- ¼ teaspoon chili powder
- ¼ teaspoon garlic powder
- 1 teaspoon vegetable oil, divided

- 2 large flour tortillas
- ¼ cup sautéed vegetables, chorizo, or filling of your choice (optional)
- Salsa, for serving
- Sour cream, for serving

TO PREPARE

1. Mix the cheeses and spices together in a medium bowl.
2. Heat ½ teaspoon of the oil in a large nonstick skillet over medium heat. Lay a tortilla in the pan, then sprinkle half of the tortilla with half of the cheese mixture and optional fillings. Fold the other half of the tortilla over, then cook for 2 to 3 minutes, until the bottom side of the quesadilla is browned. Carefully flip to brown the other side for 2 to 3 minutes, then remove from the pan and set aside.
3. Add the remaining ½ teaspoon of oil to the pan, then add the second tortilla. Sprinkle half the remaining cheese on half of the tortilla, then place the reserved quesadilla on top of the cheese. Top with the remaining cheese, then fold the bottom tortilla over to enclose all of the ingredients. Cook for 2 to 3 minutes, until the bottom side of the quesadilla is browned, then carefully flip to brown the other side for 2 to 3 minutes. Remove to a plate, slice into wedges, and enjoy with salsa and sour cream.

FRANKIE:

Would you like me to blow my courage into your mouth?

GRACE:

Thank you, no.

YOUR MOMENT OF VENN

Is your best friend a Grace, a Frankie, or somewhere in between? The kind of care they need depends on where they fall on this diagram.

GRACE

One spoonful of ice cream

Air kiss

Supportive text

Access to a label maker

Good backlighting

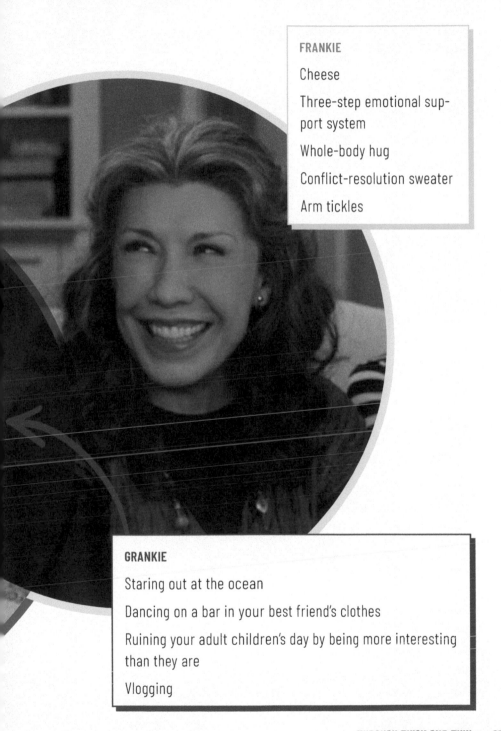

FRANKIE

Cheese

Three-step emotional support system

Whole-body hug

Conflict-resolution sweater

Arm tickles

GRANKIE

Staring out at the ocean

Dancing on a bar in your best friend's clothes

Ruining your adult children's day by being more interesting than they are

Vlogging

HOW YOU AND YOUR BEST FRIEND DEAL WITH A CRISIS

Ask for what you need.

GRACE: I need a martini.

FRANKIE: You say that a lot.

GRACE: I mean it a lot.

Stay positive.

FRANKIE: That's it. Keep going. You're doing great. Now you say it: "I'm doing great."

GRACE: You know what I'm doing great at? Keeping my hands off your throat.

Be supportive.

GRACE: Look, I'm not a coddler, OK? If I were, then I would, but I'm not, so I can't. So you have to get the hell off the floor.

Take strength from your friends.

FRANKIE: Grace, look at me. Just focus on me. Let me be your Valium. I'm Frankie Valium.

Be prepared.

FRANKIE: And if worse comes to worst, I always have Twister and four tabs of acid in the linen closet.

Do what it takes.

GRACE: Do you want to go to the art museum and touch the paintings?

FRANKIE: I did that last week.

GRACE: Come on, Frankie. I'll do anything! I'll drink beer. I'll wear a hat!

FRANKIE: A funny hat?

GRACE: Yes, a funny hat.

The Bad News Float

It happens to all of us. We get hit with that humdinger, straight between the eyes. Found out he was cheating? Ice cream required. For the last twenty years? A soup bowl full. With Robert? Add the whiskey, please (and garnish with a pack of Lucky Strikes).

INGREDIENTS

- 1 pint vanilla ice cream
- 1 (750-milliliter) bottle whiskey

TO PREPARE

Scoop out half of the ice cream into a large bowl. Add the whiskey until the bowl is half full. Enjoy! Repeat with the remaining ice cream and booze as needed.

Variation: Not feeling vanilla? Here are some other combos to get you started:

Buttered pecan ice cream with twelve-year-old Scotch

Coffee ice cream and Irish cream

Chocolate ice cream and Frangelico

Birthday cake ice cream and rye

Strawberry ice cream and white tequila

Coconut ice cream and black rum

Quick tip: Nuts are great for garnish and throwing at the TV.

Make time for your friends.

FRANKIE: You have to talk to me. It's in your planner.

GRACE: You can't just go into my planner and write "Frankie Bergstein" across Monday through Friday.

FRANKIE: Sure can. You're also scheduled for a big kiss on the mouth later.

GRACE:

I thought you were fine!
Be fine!

FRANKIE:

I am fine. During the day.
It turns out I'm less fine at
night.

GRACE:

No! You snore. You talk in
your sleep. Last night, you
kept saying, "Let's get you
out of that skin."

BEST FRIEND EMERGENCIES— HOW DO YOU RESPOND?

Scenario 1: Your bestie has fallen and she can't get up.

    a. Press the emergency button—hell, press any button you can find.

    b. Try to help her up, fall down yourself, keep repeating "It's going to be fine"—just as long as no one else sees you two like this.

Scenario 2: Earthquake!

    a. Panic. *PANIC!*

    b. Pull your friend under a table and try to avoid massaging her sternum, no matter how many times she asks you to.

Scenario 3: Your bestie is embroiled in a work disaster.

    a. Double down with ever-more-elaborate performance art to distract from your friend's failure.

    b. Craft an apology to your customers that somehow manages to smooth things over and still avoids either you or your work-wife taking any blame.

Scenario 4: Your friend's old gang is more frenemy than friend.

    a. Show up to their special brunch to mix things up. Whisper weird band-name ideas and laugh at the wrong times to unnerve everyone.

    b. Good, now you know who's on top. Give them your world-class side-eye and take them down a peg with a perfectly placed barb.

Mostly A's: You're a Frankie! In a crisis, you can sometimes be as cool as a cucumber. Other times, you're as high strung as a hummingbird in a nectar shortage. When trying to solve your friend's crisis, avoid creating new problems for them to fix.

Mostly B's: You're a Grace! You always act like you know what you're doing, because most of the time you do—except when you don't. Listen to your friend, and give her what she actually asks for sometimes. And, yes, that might include the occasional sternum massage.

"Now you get a **HEARING AID?** For years, I had to **THROW CHEESE** at you to get your attention."

—*Grace*

CHAPTER 2

TRUE WORK-MANCE

"I love spinning
your bonkers
ideas into gold."

—GRACE

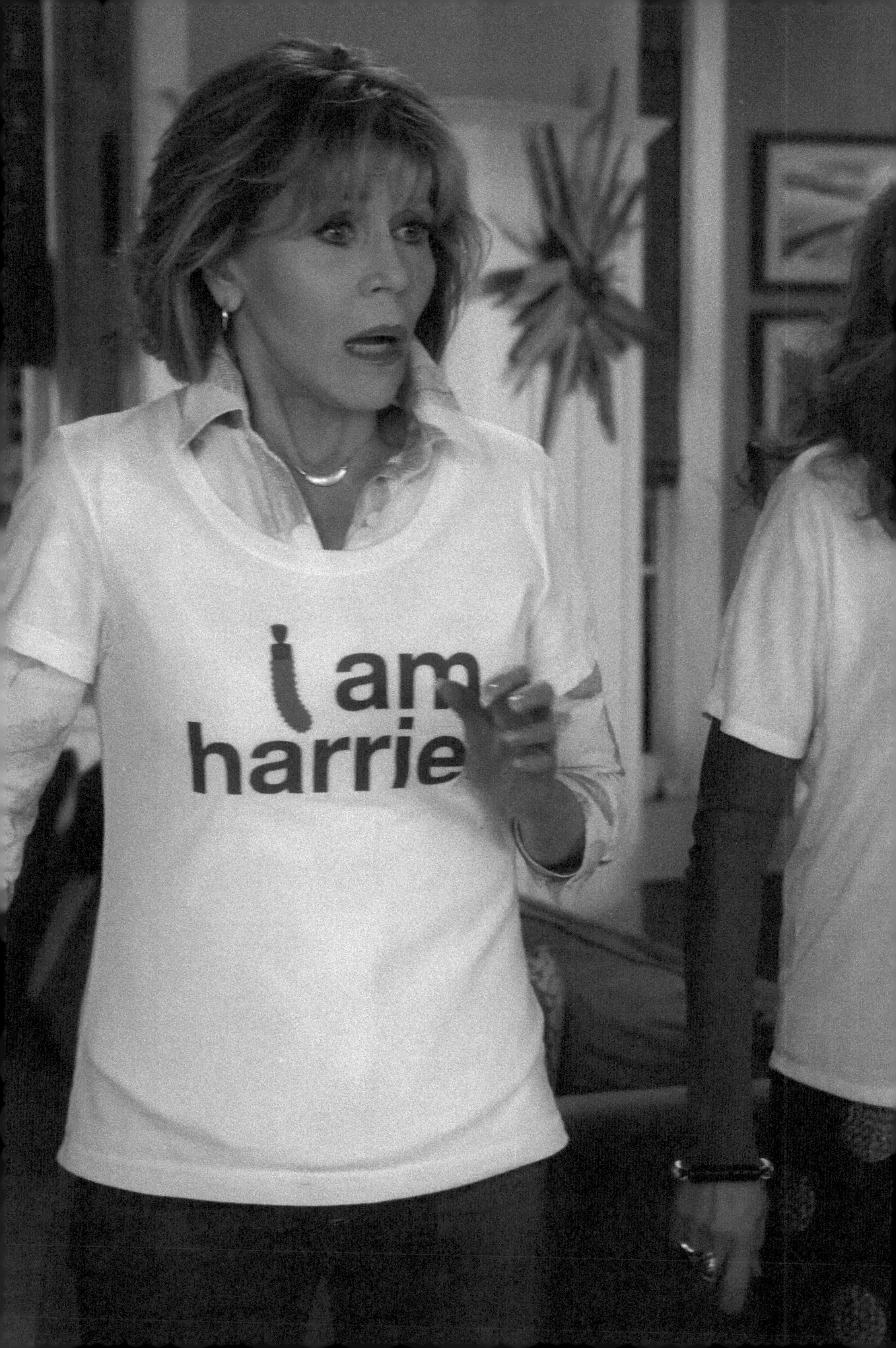
i am
harrie

While Grace and Frankie may be next-level work spouses by living and working together, their epic collaborations can inspire any workplace friendship. Whether they are developing yam-based lube for Say Grace, creating an arthritis-friendly vibrator for women of a certain age, or pitching a hydraulic toilet to *Shark Tank*, they've perfected the art of teamwork. Recognizable in any legendary start-up success story, Frankie is the visionary brainstormer to Grace's executive powerhouse—the yin to her yang, the creator of those bonkers ideas that Grace spins into gold.

Sure, things don't always go quite right. Case studies include: when Frankie promised a free vibrator and a dozen doughnuts to fifty thousand Instagram followers; when the ladies left their prototype toilet on the side of the highway; when Grace purposefully kiboshed a *Shark Tank* deal with Mark Cuban. But their combination of mad genius and mad business skills means they keep winning—dunking those entrepreneurial three-pointers and hitting ideas out of the tennis court.

It doesn't matter whether you're thirty-eight or seventy-eight—if you have a work friend who brainstorms brilliant solutions with you, elevates your ideas to the partners who like them but don't know you exist, and is always ready to spill the company tea over after-work drinks, then you might be on the road to a true Grace and Frankie work soul connection.

FRANKIE:

You're about to confront the Man, which is historically my thing.

GRACE:

I thought getting your hair stuck in the ice machine was your thing.

FRANKIE:

Hey, that was five times.

QUIZ

WHAT KIND OF WORK FRIEND ARE YOU?

1. Your friend bombs an important work presentation for both of you. All your hard work has been ruined. What do you do?

   a. Give it to them straight with a 20-slide PowerPoint. Don't let their puppy-dog eyes and mesmerizing hair trick you into forgiving them.

   b. Plan for the future—next time, you'll remember to build in time for a full-body reiki massage beforehand to help them chill out.

2. Your friend has a brilliant work idea, but no one is taking them seriously. What do you do to support them?

   a. Put on your best power suit, gather your company's leadership, and present the shit out of that idea. Your friend needs buy-in? You'll get them some goddamn buy-in.

   b. Forget asking permission—you'll just put your friend's plan into action. You know company leadership will love the idea once they see it. And if not and you both get fired . . . that's why God invented leftovers.

3. Your bestie gets overlooked for a big promotion by a supervisor known for managing up rather than looking out for their lieutenants. You:

   a. Beat the supervisor at their own game. Next opportunity, strategically remind your own boss about your bestie's value to the company. If you play your cards right, you'll both be looking at promotions.

   b. Quit alongside your friend in solidarity. Break out the shrooms and start hallucinating a new direction. Screw that job—this talking sandworm will show you both the way.

4. The staff break room is a mess. Again. Dishes in the sink, moldy food in the fridge, day-old coffee in the pot. What do you do?

    a. Post notes on every offending item and photographically document the slow decay of the food in the fridge on Instagram, tagging each of your coworkers with images of their moldy leftovers.

    b. Purify the space with a smudge stick and assume someone else will deal with it. You know Sue in accounting has a lot going on; who are you to vibe her over a few crusty bowls.

Mostly A's: You're a Grace! You use your confidence and problem-solving skills to get the job done, and no one—not even your best friend—is going to stand in the way. You won't shy away from giving them or anyone else criticism—sometimes constructive, sometimes blunt.

How to better support your Frankie: Give your friend a break and let her mess up sometimes without intervening. Indulge her in the occasional meditation session.

Mostly B's: You're a Frankie! When you get fired up, there's no stopping you—you would die for the right cause, and your best friend is always the right cause. Sometimes your solutions aren't what she would choose for herself, but you know deep down she appreciates it! And all your work friends appreciate your mellow vibe.

How to better support your Grace: Listen to your friend. Sometimes a place to vent and a problem to solve are all she needs—not your patented three-step emotional healing system.

THINGS TO KNOW WHEN STARTING A COMPANY WITH YOUR BUDDY

1. Vision boards tell the universe—and the banks—what you want.
2. Incubators aren't just for chickens anymore.
3. Listen to your friend's ideas—yes, even the one for easy-open condoms.
4. Know when to drop your easy-open condom idea and focus on your current business.
5. To save your business, sometimes the best apologies are fake ones.
6. Don't re-edit your friend's carefully crafted corporate apology in the name of honesty.
7. There is a time and a place for performance-art ketchup, and it's not a meeting with investors.
8. Sometimes you have to let your friend have control, even if you're afraid they'll sell the company for magic beans (aka tropical Skittles).
9. Learn some good business terms. "Bidding **war**"? Yes, please. "Power lunch"? Thank you, **Sharks**.
10. It's helpful to have someone to **bounce** your product name ideas **off** of.

FRANKIE:

You think I can get them to name the lube Vagicadabra? Because I have other names: "Slip Inside," "Lubri-can!," "Menapplause."

GRACE:

"Yam, Bam, Thank You, Ma'am"?

FRANKIE:

We'll throw that one in so they pick one of mine.

CEO PROFILES—CHOOSE YOURSELF AND FIND YOUR PERFECT MATCH

☐ *The Hard-Ass*

GRACE: I'm gonna shove this lawsuit so far up your fucking ass, whoever pulls it out will be crowned King Arthur!

☐ *The Self-Sacrificer*

GRACE: After great deliberation, I have decided to step down to spend less time with my family.

☐ *The Buzz Builder*

FRANKIE: We gotta shoot some fireworks off at the Safeway. It worked when I was ginning up excitement for my jug band.

☐ *The Freestyler*

GRACE: Just stick to the script.

FRANKIE: What script?

GRACE: The one I handed you yesterday, remember? I said, "Here's the script," and you said, "I don't read scripts, scripts read me," and then you sneezed in my mouth?

☐ *The Get 'Er Done*

GRACE: Get pumped, people. We need to make that deadline.

FRANKIE: Oh, now you care about deadlines? But when it's 11:55 and Del Taco's about to close, where's your concern then, Grace?

☐ *The Big Idea Person*

GRACE: Please no more half-baked ideas.

FRANKIE: Fresh baked. Real plump and fluffy.

GRACE: No. I need help with the flat, unleavened small stuff that needs to get done.

FRANKIE: I'm more of a big idea person.

☐ *The Good Cop / Bad Cop*

GRACE: This is my mistake. I'll fix it. Just follow my lead.

FRANKIE: I know, I know. Good cop, bad cop.

GRACE: No. I'm all the cops. You're a civilian ride-along.

"Not only am I an **ARTIST**, I'm a **BUSINESSWOMAN**. I'm a hyphenate. Or a **SLASH**. What do you think?"

—*Frankie*

DOS AND DON'TS FOR WORKING WITH YOUR BESTIE

By Frankie Annotated by Grace

1. Do remember where things belong.

   The TV remote does <u>not</u> go in the cordless phone base, Frankie.

2. ~~Do~~ Don't take short naps during meetings.

3. Do share new ideas whenever you think of them!

   Save all new ideas for 10:15 -10:20 a.m.

4. Don't have breakfast in the workspace conference room.

   And keep your mouth closed when eating veggie bacon and muffins.

5. Do watch for traffic . . . on the stairs.

   This is not a thing.

6. Do wear clogs for any occasion.

   If your feet aren't hurting, you're not trying hard enough.

7. Do start the workday ~~by noon.~~ at <u>8:30 a.m.</u>

8. Don't worry about job security: no one can fire you.

   Oh really? Watch me.

9. Do steal the office supplies.

   They're already yours.

Frankie's Doughnuts

When we get ourselves in tight spots, our best friends don't judge. They do keep us from executing our worst bright ideas—like these homemade doughnuts.

INGREDIENTS

- 1 egg
- A dozen pumpernickel bagels
- A dozen plain bagels
- 1 cup powdered sugar
- Sprinkles

TO PREPARE

1. Preheat oven to 300 degrees F.
2. Beat the egg with 1 tablespoon of water.
3. Brush the egg wash evenly over the bagels.
4. Place the powdered sugar and sprinkles in individual shallow bowls. Dip the egg-washed side of the pumpernickel bagels into the powdered sugar and place onto a baking sheet. Repeat with the plain bagels and the sprinkles.
5. Bake for 10 minutes to set the toppings. Enjoy!

A TIP FROM GRACE

Life's too short for all-nighters.

GRACE: Frankie, this is not a problem that can be solved by one Mountain Dew–fueled all-night bake-o-rama.

GRACE:

You're late for work. Again.

FRANKIE:

Um, I'm on London time.

GRACE:

Then you're eight hours late.

Always consult a trusted friend before you act.

GRACE: Why didn't you talk to me first, before you did something crazy?

FRANKIE: I did. I did a whole role play up in my studio. And you really agreed with me.

Frankie's Yam ~~Lube~~ Butter

A true friend doesn't judge what you use your yam butter for, but this kind is definitely for putting on toast.

INGREDIENTS

- 4 medium yams or sweet potatoes, unpeeled, cut into chunks
- ½ cup apple cider or juice
- ¼ cup honey
- 1 teaspoon cinnamon
- ½ teaspoon ground ginger
- Pinch ground nutmeg
- Pinch ground cloves

TO PREPARE

1. Put the yams in a steamer basket and cook over boiling water until soft.
2. Add the yams to a blender along with the rest of the ingredients. Start on low speed and gradually increase until pureed. Be careful with the hot liquid!
3. Pour the mixture into a saucepan and put it back on the stove and simmer until thick, about 15 to 20 minutes.
4. Ladle into jars. The yam butter keeps in the fridge for about a month.

FRANKIE:

Sounds like our target market.

GRACE:

Target market? You're throwing around a lot of fancy terms lately.

FRANKIE:

I googled "business words."

CHAPTER 3

REAL FRIENDS FIGHT

"That little girl is still in you . . . I see her all the time. When you're giving me shit for being a sucky navigator or you're chucking towels and hats at me."

—FRANKIE

Friendships aren't all heart emojis and vagina balloons. Sometimes your bestie goes on a bender and tells your new boyfriend you're afraid of sex in the vagina; other times, they may blow your chances for business success by refusing to back down from promising vibrators and doughnuts to tens of thousands of women. Then there are the times when your best friend destroys your kitchen ceiling tie-dyeing a bathtub full of T-shirts, and that time she ran off to Vegas to marry her billionaire boyfriend without even telling you.

At any rate, a close friendship can be really hard sometimes. Like the best romance, it can take work, humility, and pure endurance. But if you are in a true friendship, when push comes to shove, you share the talking stick (or avoid all hard conversation), smoke a bowl (or have a few drinks), and go to bed besties. (No, you can't sleep with me again, Frankie.)

If you or your best friend has criticized the other's parenting style, fashion choices, or business acumen and then felt like a complete asshole in the morning, remember that if Grace and Frankie can forgive each other for the shit they've done, you can, too.

HOW DO YOU FRIEND-FIGHT?

Choose Your Preferred Method.

☐ *The backhanded compliment:*

FRANKIE: All those years, I thought you were stuck-up and boring as shit. But it turns out you were stuck-up and interesting as shit.

☐ *The dramatic flair:*

GRACE: Would you mind taking me back home or setting me on fire?

☐ *The old-timey insult:*

GRACE: You play like an Amish kid!

☐ *The comparison:*

FRANKIE: I'm just like you, but with a better personality!

☐ *The guilt trip:*

FRANKIE: Your anger is frightening the sand.

☐ *The redirect:*

GRACE: Frankie, you need to find a way to calm down!

FRANKIE: No, you need to find a way to calm down about me not calming down!

☐ *The personal attack:*

FRANKIE: You might want to get your head out of your collar and accept that everything is going to change.

"I'm **NOT** going to get into the weeds with you on 'booming' versus 'blasting.' **AGAIN**."

—*Grace*

HOW TO DELIVER A SCATHING COMEBACK LINE

The I-know-you-are-but-what-am-I:

FRANKIE: You know how I felt when you were gone? Free. You think you're the "Wind Beneath My Wings"? I am my own *Beaches*.

GRACE: No, I am my own *Beaches*. And I don't even know what that means!

The dramatic exit:

FRANKIE: Why is everyone on my case today?

GRACE: Well, maybe you should take a good, long look at that.

FRANKIE: Oh, you're not storming out. I'm storming out.

GRACE: No, I'm storming out, and I know exactly where I'm going.

FRANKIE: So do I . . . Excuse me, do you know where I can find a map . . .

The tell-it-like-it-is:

FRANKIE: J'accuse! Which means—

GRACE: I know what it means. It means you got too stoned again and tried to even out with too much coffee.

The literalist approach:

GRACE: How . . . how can you say that?

FRANKIE: My brain sends a message to my mouth and it comes out. Neurology, Grace.

The I-don't-think-so:

FRANKIE: If it's any consolation, I've been just awful with myself in my diary.

GRACE: You mean your bullshit diary where you write in the air?

The shows-what-you-know:

GRACE: You do seven things a day I ask you not to!

FRANKIE: I actually do more. You only catch seven.

The take <u>that</u>:

GRACE: You think you're sooo clever. Well, two can play at that game. Number one, I flushed your geodes and broke your toilet. And number two . . . I have a valid driver's license and money. I can get booze anywhere. You want more geodes, you're going to have to drive to Borrego and wait for Gary to open his stand.

The ultimate comeback line:

FRANKIE: I have an amazing comeback to that, but I can't say it because I'm not talking to you.

YOUR ROOMIE EATS YOUR FOOD FROM THE FRIDGE— WHAT'S YOUR MOVE?

Scrounge up some vindaloo from your nightstand—you probably left some basmati in the dryer.

Tell her it's gluten- and dairy-free. She won't touch it.

At least she didn't find the vodka.

Reveal that it's actually your homemade lube.

Give her a Del-Talking to.

Joke's on them—you don't actually eat food anyway.

■ You're a Grace!
■ You're a Frankie!

FRANKIE:

Can I get you something?

GRACE:

A larger sphere of personal space.

FRANKIE:

It's the one thing I'm out of.

GRACE:

Then, no.

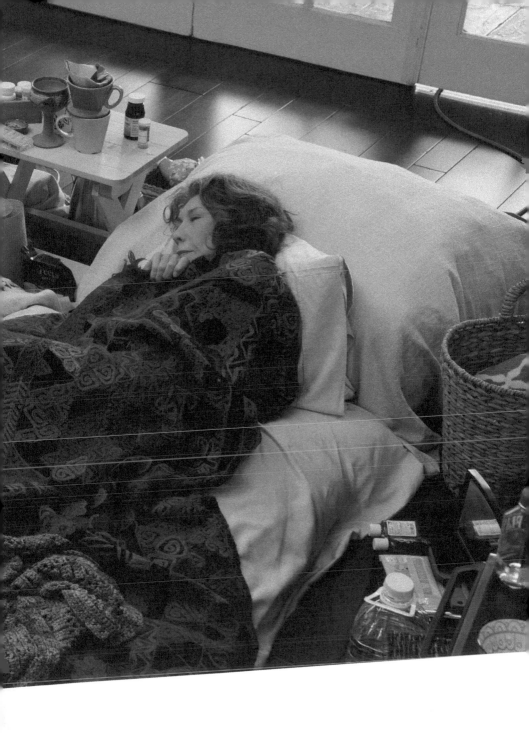

HOW TO FESS UP
AFTER YOU MESS UP

Apologize:

FRANKIE: I—I—didn't know it was a secret?

GRACE: Of course you did!

Try again:

FRANKIE: I have poor impulse control. It's always been a problem.

GRACE: Oh, please.

FRANKIE: It's true. I was once a shoo-in to win the giant produce contest at the fair in Del Mar, but I caved and ate the zucchini in the car on the way over. It's a condition. Like irritable bowel syndrome.

OK, one more time:

FRANKIE: Come on, you were dying to tell me. And by the way, secrets are bad for you. They can give you fibroids. Or is that grief eating? Either way, they're extremely toxic.

Seriously, last chance:

FRANKIE: I'm going to make it up to you.

GRACE: You're moving out?

FRANKIE: I owe you the most embarrassing secret
   I have. And you can tell whoever you want.

Grace's Vodka Watermelon

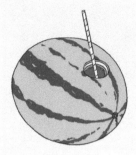

Sometimes you need to talk it out, and sometimes you need to drown it out. Drink your feelings and get your vitamins by combining your vodka with watermelon, a fruit so low-calorie, Frankie says it's "basically celery in a Lilly Pulitzer dress."

INGREDIENTS (IN ORDER OF IMPORTANCE)
- 1 (750-millileter) bottle vodka
- 1 ripe watermelon

TO PREPARE
1. If you have one, use a pineapple corer to take a plug out of the watermelon. If you don't, take a sharp, thin knife and carefully make a hole roughly the diameter of the neck of the bottle, cutting through to the center of the melon and removing the flesh. (Bonus: think of *him* while you're stabbing the fruit.) *(WARNING: Stabbing a melon with a knife can be dangerous—exercise caution.)*
2. Open the bottle of vodka and insert it into the hole. Leave to drain into the fruit.
3. Remove the bottle and take the watermelon with you to your room. Let it "marinate" as long as you can before having at it with a straw and a spoon.

Don't try so hard.

FRANKIE: Did I just see you and Sheree do a *Top Gun* high-five? I've been trying to do a *Top Gun* high-five with you for years.

GRACE: With her, it's natural. You want it too much.

"I would **NEVER** wish anything **BAD** on him. Other than the time I wished something bad on him."

—*Frankie*

FRANKIE:

What are you freaking out about? Break down your emotions for me.

GRACE:

Annoyance. Irritation—

FRANKIE:

No, that's how you're feeling about me.

Yes, even a sharing circle has rules.

GRACE: OK. That's it! We're doing a sharing circle.

FRANKIE: Shows how much you know. You can't do a sharing circle with two people.

Frankie's Fondue

Communal cheese can grease the wheels of so many occasions. Setting up your friend with that perfect someone? Fondue! Sol calls it "the ultimate conversation starter." Best friend fight? Break out the pot and those cute tiny forks because, as Frankie says, "you can't keep fighting when you're sharing a cheese fondue!"

INGREDIENTS

- 1 clove garlic
- 4 cups (about 1 pound) freshly grated cheese (Gruyere and Swiss are good choices)
- 1½ tablespoons cornstarch
- 1½ cups dry white wine (you know where the rest of the bottle goes)
- 2 tablespoons cherry brandy (one for the fondue and one for you)

TO PREPARE

1. Peel the garlic clove and cut it in half. Rub the inside of a fondue pot with the garlic, then toss it aside like all those angry feelings.
2. In a large bowl, toss the cheese with the cornstarch and set aside.
3. Place the wine and the brandy in the fondue pot and set over a can of Sterno or a hot plate. Bring to a simmer.
4. Slowly add in the cheese, a bit at a time, waiting until each addition has melted before adding more and stirring gently all the while. Isn't that meditative?
5. Serve with vegetables, bread cubes, pickles . . . really anything within spearing range.

CHAPTER 4

ROMANCE IS OVER-RATED

"Soul mate! Now there is a meaningless concept."

—GRACE

Grace and Frankie have been the ultimate rebound friends since their husbands of forty years dumped them in tandem over a seafood tower. Things seemed bleak, but with a figurative—and literal—"fuck you," they got the last laugh: claiming the to-die-for beach house and kicking off their life together with an epic peyote journey.

Since that night on the beach (aka the desert with water), they've been there for each other through every blind date, love affair, and destined-for-heartbreak reunion. They've followed love all the way to Mission Viejo and Santa Fe, but always stayed true to their friendship. They've been there for each other through the big highs and the low lows, and they've cried on each other's shoulders. And as Grace once said (while on a vision quest, naturally): there was a whole world in those tears.

If you are lucky enough to have a Frankie in your life, you already know they'll loan you their best chunky necklace (whether you want it or not) for a big date, and will be there with a cookie-dough-filled pineapple when his idea of dinner conversation is telling you about his fatty lipoma with teeth. If you've got a Grace as your best friend, you know they'll give it to you straight when you're on the wrong path, but if things fall apart, they will be the first person to help you get through a lonely night via walkie-talkie. From ex-husbands to one-night stands to fiancés and new husbands, Grace and Frankie prove that romantic entanglements don't become less complicated with age, but friends last forever.

TIPS FOR DEALING WITH YOUR BESTIE'S ANNOYING SIGNIFICANT OTHER

Frankie recommends:

1. Break out the cheeba twenty minutes before he arrives, and then every hour on the hour
2. Invite him to see your newest vagina self-portrait
3. Schedule your Tuvan throat singing group for a double practice at your place
4. Meditate silently with your eyes open
5. Voodoo doll

Grace suggests:

1. Dry vodka martini
2. Ignore
3. Deny
4. Deflect
5. Did I already say vodka?

HOW DO YOU HELP YOUR BESTIE DEAL WITH THESE COMMON DATING MISTAKES?

Mistake 1: It was an Ambien breakup: Your friend broke it off with someone, but their significant other was sleepwalking when it happened and has no memory of the breakup. What should your friend do now?

   a. Do it once more, with feeling.

   b. Fake their own death—it's easier than you might think to be declared legally dead.

Mistake 2: Slept with an ex: A moment of weakness or a bid for closure—whatever you want to call it, it happened. What should your friend do?

   a. Take ownership. Tell the truth, take the fall, and pour a double.

   b. Keep the secret until they just can't keep it anymore—then blurt away, consequences be damned!

Mistake 3: Accidentally stood up their date—twice: When your friend has a lot going on, sometimes romance takes a back seat. What should they do to keep a sputtering flame alight?

   a. Flirt like their life depends on it—even if it means they look like they're having a stroke.

   b. Make it up to their date with a romantic evening talking about seed varietals while eating a tagine made of surplus vegetables.

Mistake 4: Kissed an ex-con in the kitchen: There's only so much smolder a person can take before they find themselves kissing an artistic ex-con with a passion for ham sandwiches. What's your advice?

   a. Kiss them again!

   b. Better make it two ham sandwiches.

Mistake 5: Agreed to a date with a lonely sea captain: That yachtchitect sounded so much better in his profile . . . What's your friend's next move when Ahab shows up at brunch?

   a. Sink that ship.

   b. Stick around for the eggs Benedict, then gently shove him back out to sea.

Mistake 6: Tried to date two people at once: It's not two-timing, it's one-at-a-timing with two people. But you know it can only last so long. What should your friend do?

   a. Come clean—let them both know what's going on before it all goes to hell.

   b. See it through until it blows up, then enjoy double dumplings when they get double dumped.

Mostly A's: You're a Grace! You may hit snags in your own love life, but you've got your friend's love life sorted. Now if only they would take your fashion advice, too.

Mostly B's: You're a Frankie! Love is complicated and squishy, just like you. You always remind your friend that no matter what happens, you'll be there to tell them how great they are and offer them a smoothie to cheer them up, even if they don't want it—maybe especially if they don't want it; you know what's best for them.

How to Get Your Grace Back into Her Heels

1. Tell her she's beautiful
2. Actually, tell her she's a stone-cold fox
3. Tell her she scares you a little, but in a good way
4. Tell her she doesn't look a day over fifty-three
5. Give her an idea for a new business venture to take her mind off things
6. Have margaritas waiting . . . but don't bother unless you have fresh-squeezed lime
7. Hug her, but do it without touching
8. Give back the pile of stuff you stole from her
9. Remind her how much better she is than every person she's ever dated

How to Give Your Frankie the Support She Needs

1. Offer ample hugs
2. Get lost in the forest together
3. Comfort her with healing crystals
4. Join her in expressing your feelings through art
5. Pass the talking stick
6. Smudge the beach house
7. Commune with helpful spirits
8. Do a vision board together
9. If nothing is working, throw weed at the problem

"I was **MARRIED BY A CULT LEADER** like a normal person. I didn't just fly off in the middle of the night **WITHOUT TELLING ANYONE.**"

—*Frankie*

Frankie's 5 Best Parts of Being Single

1. You get Ray Donovan all to yourself
2. No one accuses you of bogarting the joint
3. You can stop eating yams for every meal
4. You have time to paint that mural of yourself transforming into a lemur
5. You can sit on a park bench with your best friend's daughter and watch people fall into a puddle

Grace's 5 Best Parts of Being Single

1. No one asks you how it feels to date someone who ate their travel companion
2. You don't have to pretend to like golf or hoagies
3. You don't have to make conversation with anyone else's second wife at dinner parties (who is guaranteed to be fifty years younger than you)
4. More time for work
5. You can choose your own couch

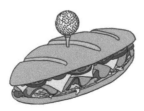

HOW DO YOU GIVE DATING ADVICE TO YOUR BESTIE?

Choose All that Apply:

☐ *Deliver practical step-by-step instructions.*

GRACE: Men love it when women mimic their physical behavior. And laugh at what they say.

FRANKIE: Let me get a piece of paper.

GRACE: Oh, and tilt your head slightly to the side.

FRANKIE: Why?

GRACE: To show deep interest in what he's saying!

FRANKIE: You mean like my retriever used to do?

GRACE: Exactly.

☐ *Help them break out of their rut.*

FRANKIE: Soooooo? Did you sign up for the dating site I signed you up for?

GRACE: Yes. And oddly enough, I did not find the love of my life on HippieRoundup.com.

☐ *Give them a pep talk.*

GRACE: What does it matter? I blew it. It's over.

FRANKIE: It's not over. This is just the part of the movie where you have to run through the airport.

GRACE: I don't really have the knees for that.

□ *Suggest a good pickup line.*

GRACE: When you go on these things, you generally start off with a cute anecdote about yourself. I use the one about nursing a baby bird back to health.

FRANKIE: That was me!

GRACE: Yeah, I took that. It's a big hit, should you ever start dating.

□ *Have them casually bump into their ex with a handsome new date.*

FRANKIE: Ohhh. I see what you're doing. An "accidental" meeting. Erica Kane did that to Dimitri Marick on *All My Children*. Someone ended up dying. And then coming back as a twin. And then dying again in a grain silo. I like it.

□ *Prepare them for the worst.*

GRACE: But what if he's a flat-earther, or a dog kicker?

FRANKIE: Nah, I asked him point-blank if he kicks dogs.

GRACE: OK, what if he doesn't believe in aliens?

FRANKIE: You shut your mouth.

□ *Tell them you'll always be there for them.*

GRACE: But, Frankie, if I break up with him, there is a good chance I will be by myself for the rest of my life. And I know you're going to be here, but I can't stand the thought of waking up every day alone.

FRANKIE: I could wake you up.

GRACE: Maybe it's more about falling asleep in someone's arms.

FRANKIE: I could do that, too. But you wouldn't like it.

(continued)

☐ *Try some tough love.*

FRANKIE: This is what you do. You stand up. You put your damn purse on your arm the way you like it. And you do exactly what you told me to do with Jacob.

GRACE: What did I tell you to do with Jacob?

FRANKIE: "Don't be an idiot."

GRACE: That does sound like me . . .

☐ *Or maybe some not-so-tough love.*

GRACE: I spent forty years with a man who didn't love me. Maybe I was the problem. Maybe I'm unlovable.

FRANKIE: You're not unlovable.

GRACE: You sure?

FRANKIE: Now you're fishin', and guess what? Ya caught one. I love you. Happy?

Success!

Grace's Very Dry Martini*

Whether she's steeling herself for dinner with her perpetually disappointing family, dodging Frankie's exploration into phallic finger-painting, or killing time while stuck on a suspiciously uncomfortable Italian couch, a vodka martini is Grace's favorite sidekick. While her trademark is the dry vodka martini—otherwise known as a couple shots of vodka in a nice glass—add vermouth to taste. Because as Grace says, "alcohol has its own rules."

INGREDIENTS

- 2½ ounces top-shelf vodka (preferably not made from potatoes, because who needs those carbs?)
- ½ ounce vermouth (optional)
- Ice
- 2 olives

TO PREPARE

Combine the vodka and vermouth, if using, with ice in a cocktail shaker. Shake vigorously for 10 seconds, and then strain into a chilled martini glass. Olives take up room in your glass that could be vodka, so put those to the side. They will be your dinner. Serve.

(for consolation, or for throwing in someone's face)

Always tell your friend when she has something in her teeth or on her face.

GRACE: How long has that been there? How many times do I have to tell you? If you see something, say something.

YOUR FRIEND IS GOING TO SEE HER EX AT A SOCIAL EVENT— HOW DO YOU HELP HER?

Choose Your Preferred Method.

☐ Find your friend a dress that makes her ass look amazing. Everyone should be thinking "What a waste" when she walks into the room. (Or when she walks out of it, actually.)

☐ Go with your bestie for moral support. The two of you can sit in the corner and make snide remarks about her ex's date.

☐ Help your friend stuff her feelings deep down with a box of Cheez-Its.

☐ Find the perfect revenge date for your friend to bring. Bonus points if they're tall and can reach onto high shelves, or small and can fit through dog doors.

☐ Send your regrets and make plans with your bestie for an epic "say yes" night.

☐ Tell her to write her feelings in the sand. Then write your feelings about her feelings in the sand.

■ You're a Grace!

■ You're a Frankie!

FRANKIE:

OK, well, he's wrong for you on every level.

GRACE:

Why? Because he doesn't have a car that runs on millet?

Always go out with a bang.

FRANKIE: When he breaks up with you, you know
what to tell him?

GRACE: He has herpes?

FRANKIE: He has herpes.

Retribution Shrimp

Your best friend knows that sometimes acting like a lady involves throwing food, even if everyone's looking.

INGREDIENTS

- ½ pound chilled poached shrimp
- Lemon wedge, for garnish

TO PREPARE

1. Plate the shrimp and garnish with the lemon.
2. Grab handfuls and throw, aiming for the head.

"This joint is chockablock with **OLD GEEZERS** who would jump at the chance to marry a **BEAUTIFUL WOMAN** with all her hair and **TEN GRAND.**"

—*Frankie*

CHAPTER 5

GOOD FRIENDS LAST FOREVER

"You make me feel strong, Grace Hanson, like I could do anything."

—FRANKIE

A true-blue friend is that person who elevates you, allowing you to be the very best Grace or Frankie you can be. Whether you are golf-cart commandeering, hot-air-balloon riding, or beach-bonfire dancing, a best-friendship is one that makes you all the better for being part of a duo.

Your Grace or Frankie is the friend who convinces you to trade clothes, dance on a bar, and accept flights of tequila from middle-aged lotharios; the friend who gives you the confidence to start three businesses in your seventies (and still trusts you after you do your best to torch all three); and the friend with whom you break out of a retirement community. She knows where you stash your emergency candy or your emergency vodka. She sees past your brick-with-cement-mortar emotional walls, and knows just the right next move, even if it may not seem like the right—or legal—thing to do at the time.

Grace without Frankie might be just another bored retired CEO with an immovable face and too much time on her hands. Frankie without Grace might be just another bong-toking grandma with multicolored dreadlocks. But together, they take on the world.

So, celebrate the Thelma to your Louise. Make the best of every day you've got together, because at the end of it all, she is the wind beneath your wings and she will always be your *Beaches*. As Grace once said, "Ever since you and I became you and me, we've done a lot of crazy shit, but we've always done it together."

WHAT'S YOUR PERFECT FRIEND DATE?

☐ Fro-yo—especially if Brian's working

☐ Working lunch

☐ Paint your auras (or maybe vaginas?)

☐ Martinis at a nice bar. Or a Cheesecake Factory. Or a colonoscopy. Or the zoo. Or one of Robert's plays.

☐ Video bowling—in a tailored outfit

☐ Create custom blends of herbal tea that help align your chakras

☐ Get stoned and go out for all-you-can-eat crab legs

■ You're a Grace!

■ You're a Frankie!

FRANKIE:

How can I be the cool one in the relationship with a hearing aid? Besides, they've never once gone with my outfit. Now, an ear trumpet, on the other hand . . .

GRACE:

What do you mean? You're always the cool one in a relationship. You told me yourself.

FRANKIE:

Grace, I tell you lots of things.

HOW TO FREAK OUT YOUR GROWN CHILDREN

1. Talk about your dry vagina
2. Accidentally drive their infant to Tijuana
3. Start three businesses in the time it takes them to almost lose one
4. Have more sex than they do
5. Tell them to make their own fucking sandwiches
6. Squat in the house they sold out from under you
7. Steal an ambulance golf cart to break out of your residential living community
8. Offer to be the doula at the homebirth of their child
9. Always be ten times smarter than they are

HOW WELL DO YOU KNOW YOUR FRIEND?

Choose All that Apply:

☐ *You know how they take their coffee.*

GRACE: I'm going to get us some coffee.

FRANKIE: Will you—

GRACE: I will ask if they can put ice cream in it.

☐ *They hide nothing from you.*

GRACE: How could you not tell me this?

FRANKIE: Grace, I'm a private person.

GRACE: You're the least private person in the world! The first time I met you, you yanked up your shirt and said, "Do these things look right to you?"

☐ *And we mean <u>nothing</u>.*

FRANKIE: There have been many Frankies, as it turns out . . . in this lifetime alone.

GRACE: With many vaginas. There are four more here than I ever needed to see.

☐ *You anticipate their every move.*

GRACE: So I'll meet you at the airport three flights after the one we're supposed to be on.

FRANKIE: I feel so known.

☐ *You can really relax around each other.*

GRACE: God, I love being able to, you know, drop it all.

FRANKIE: Right? And just relax. And pass gas.

GRACE: Please don't pass gas.

FRANKIE: OK, starting . . . now.

☐ *You can't bear to be apart.*

FRANKIE: What are you so afraid of?

GRACE: Waking up and not seeing your hats in the dishwasher. Not hearing you singing "Kriss Kross will make you jump jump" from your studio. Never again cringing at your borderline-offensive Jamaican accent.

FRANKIE: Why do you think this decision has been so hard for me? I would miss your love of color-coding spices, how you try so hard to be funny. The way you can always find my purse.

TOP TEN RULES FOR THE ROAD

1. If it's farther than your doctor's office, it counts as a road trip
2. Channel your inner teenage self for guidance
3. If you stay on the shoulder, it's OK to drive twenty miles below the speed limit
4. Drive on any road (except the freeway)
5. Stop yelling at me when I'm trying to merge!
6. When the traffic signs are in a different language, you've gone too far
7. While driving under the influence is a no, taking your driving test under the influence is a yes
8. A restricted license is more license than none
9. Stop at every drive-thru you see
10. Swap the car for a hot-air balloon

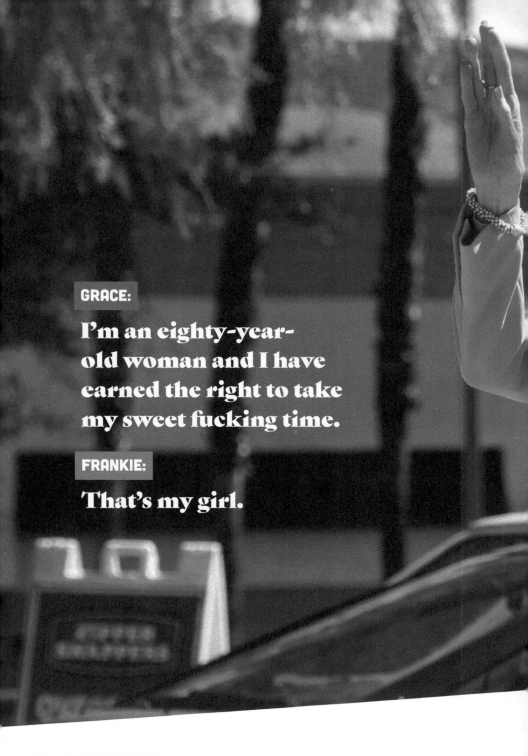

GRACE:

I'm an eighty-year-old woman and I have earned the right to take my sweet fucking time.

FRANKIE:

That's my girl.

Frankie's Cake-Yata

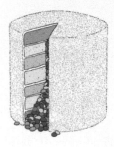

For true celebrations of friendship, the cake-yata offers all the taste of a cake with the fun of a piñata!

INGREDIENTS

- 4 boxes white cake mix
- Blue, green, orange, and red food coloring
- 4 tubs white frosting
- 2 bags Skittles
- 2 containers multicolored sprinkles

TO PREPARE

1. Preheat the oven to 350 degrees F. Butter and flour as many 9-inch cake pans as you have. You will be baking seven cake layers in all.

2. Prepare the cake batter as directed, dividing it into four separate bowls. Remove half the batter from one of the bowls and discard.

3. To the bowl with half the batter, add enough food coloring to make a vibrant deep blue. Repeat with the other colors in the remaining bowls of batter until you have festive blue, green, orange, and deep pink.

4. Place the blue batter in one cake pan. Divide each remaining bowl of batter between two cake pans. If you don't have enough pans, just bake them in batches. Bake according to package directions or until a toothpick inserted in the middle comes out clean. Turn out each layer onto a wire rack and cool completely.

5. Place a small amount of frosting on a cardboard round and place one pink layer on top. Spread a thin layer of frosting on top of the pink layer. Top with a green layer.

6. Repeat the process so that the layers are in the following order, starting from the bottom: pink, green, orange, blue, orange, green. (Don't place the final pink layer yet.)

7. Trace a 4-inch-diameter circle in the middle of the green layer. Using a sharp knife, cut out the middle of the cake and remove. Pour the Skittles into the hole. Top with the final pink layer, then frost the top and sides of the cake with the remaining frosting. While the frosting is still soft, coat the outside of the cake with the sprinkles.

8. To serve, cut with a knife (not a bat).

FRANKIE:

Are you forgetting how we became best friends? I wore you down. I didn't leave. I squatted you, Grace.

GRACE:

Oh God, you did.

Grace's Road Trip Bloody Marys

If your bestie is driving (and you live in certain states), enjoy Grace's favorite car snack—a thermos of Bloody Marys. Ingredients are for one "normal" drink. Double, triple, wait . . . multiply everything by ten and stir it up in a pitcher before filling your thermos. Now you're ready to hit the open road.

INGREDIENTS

- 1½ ounces vodka
- ½ teaspoon freshly grated horseradish
- ¼ cup tomato juice
- A few dashes Tabasco

TO PREPARE

Place all ingredients in a tall ice-filled glass. Stir together with a celery stick.

Variation: To make a "Butch" Bloody Mary, sometimes the drink the occasion requires, use the same recipe, just omit the horseradish, the tomato juice, and the hot sauce.

GRACE:

So, how did this "say yes" night measure up?

FRANKIE:

Grace, we got kicked out of a bar and my Leaf got towed. That immediately puts it into the top five.

A TIP FROM FRANKIE

Stick together at all costs.

FRANKIE: Bad things happen when we split up. That's how this whole mess started. Also how the grill ended up at the bottom of the pool last Memorial Day.

There are exceptions to every rule.

FRANKIE: Can there be balloons? Vagina balloons?

GRACE: For the first time ever, my answer to that question is yes.

FRANKIE:

You know what? You're first-rate, kid.

GRACE:

You're first-rate, too, Frankie.

ACKNOWLEDGMENTS

Our heartfelt thanks to:

Co-creators Marta Kauffman and Howard J. Morris; Skydance Television including Executive Producers David Ellison, Dana Goldberg, and Bill Bost along with Katherine Morrison; Okay Goodnight including Executive Producer Robbie Tollin along with Hannah KS Canter; Executive Producers Paula Weinstein and Marcy Ross; Kirsti Tichenor and Travis Rutherford at Evolution; and the cast and crew of *Grace and Frankie*.

CPSIA information can be obtained
at www.ICGtesting.com
Printed in the USA
LVHW051528280821
696346LV00005B/5

9 781736 324387